THE POWER OF PRAYER

By

Pastor James Justin

Dr. Lauretta Justin

Copyright © 2016 by James & Lauretta Justin

THE POWER OF PRAYER

By James Justin & Dr. Lauretta Justin

Printed in the United States of America

ISBN-10: 0-9971126-4-6
ISBN-13: 978-0-9971126-4-1

Book Industry Standards and Communications (BISAC) Categories: 1. Religion & Spirituality 2. Inspirational 3. Christian Books & Bibles 4. Christian Living 5. Spiritual Growth

Keywords: Prayer, Pray, Benefits of Prayer, Spiritual Health, Relationship with God, Christian, Faith

All rights reserved solely by the author. The author guarantees all contents are original and do not infringe upon the legal rights of any other person or work. No part of this book may be reproduced in any form without written permission of the author. The views in this book are not necessarily those of the publisher.

Unless otherwise indicated, Bible quotations are taken from the New King James Version (NKJV) of the Bible. Copyright © 1982 by Thomas Nelson, Inc.; The Amplified Bible (AMP). Copyright © 1954, 1958, 1962, 1964, 1965, 1987 by the Lockman Foundation; The Contemporary English Version, (CEV). Copyright © 1995 American Bible Society; The New Living Translation copyright © 1996, 2004, 2007 by Tyndale House Foundation and The New International Version®, (NIV®). Copyright © 1973, 1978, 1984, 2011 by Biblica, Inc.

To contact the authors, visit CoachJamesJustin.com

6601 Old Winter Garden Rd.
Suite 104
Orlando, FL 32835

Products by the Authors

- 12 Tips to Achieve your Financial Freedom: The Simple Guide to Successfully Manage your Personal Finance by James Justin

- 7 Steps to Develop Healthy Relationships with Anyone by James Justin

- Mindset: How to transform your life from ordinary to extraordinary by James Justin

- Positive Parenting: 12 Tips to prepare your kids for success by James Justin

- Parenting Digital Natives: What parents can do about the danger of social media and online activities of their kids by Dr. Lauretta Justin

- Christian Counseling by James Justin and Dr. Lauretta Justin

- The Power of Prayer by James Justin and Dr. Lauretta Justin

- CEO OF YOU: How to Create the Business and the Life of Your Dreams by Dr. Lauretta Justin

- The Spirit of Christmas (Music CD) by Dr. Lauretta Justin

Visit CoachJamesJustin.com to get any of our latest products!

Dedication

To our parents: Mr. Julien J. Justin and Mrs. Marie P. Justin (James' parents).

Mr. Esperance Seide and Mrs. Maxia Seide (Lauretta's parent).

Thank you for your love and sacrifices to help us succeed in life. We are grateful and honor you!

Acknowledgement

To our editor and friend, Mark Wahlton, thank you for your partnership!

Table of Contents

INTRODUCTION 1
Chapter 1. WHAT IS PRAYER? 5
Chapter 2. THE PURPOSE OF PRAYER 13
Chapter 3. THE POWER OF PRAYER 33
Chapter 4. THE LORD'S PRAYER 49
Chapter 5. THE 3 KEYS TO EFFECTIVE PRAYER 61
Chapter 6. TOP 20 PRAYERS OF ALL TIME 79
CONCLUSION 119
NOTES 121
ABOUT THE AUTHORS 129

INTRODUCTION

Did you know you can talk to God anytime and anywhere? Yes, you can! It is as easy as talking with your best friend. If you can talk for hours with your best friend, you can do the same with God. You do not have to wait until you have a crisis. You can start today. It will not be a burden once you understand prayer and develop a personal relationship with God.

Prayer is a form of communication. Effective communication is the primary step in building strong relationships. In order to develop a strong relationship with God, you need to communicate with Him. There are many ways to communicate with God; however, prayer is the simplest form. Prayer allows you to express your heart's desires to the Creator of the universe. It gives human beings the ability to reach beyond the stars. Prayer is powerful! It can change your life and the lives of those around you. If you desire to strengthen your relationship with God through prayer, this is the right book for you. This book offers practical keys on how to develop an intimate relationship with God.

Prayer is a vast subject; it is impossible to cover its entirety in one book. However, what we have learned by the grace of God through study and research, we will teach you in a practical way. Although there are many books written on the subject, this book presents prayer in a simple, in a practical and in a relevant way. Whether you are a new Christian, have been a Christian for many years or are simply curious on this subject, you will be able to read, understand and apply the principles of this book in your daily life. We encourage you to give a copy of this book to your loved ones. It will change their lives.

And although it is just as easy to talk to God as it is talking with your spouse or best friend, in some cases it may be easier to speak with God because He knows your thoughts and feelings. Since He already knows your deepest thoughts and attitudes, you do not have to spend a lot of energy trying to find the right words; He understands how you feel even before you express it. Therefore, feel free to tell God what is on your mind!

He will not reject you. He loves you and wants to hear from you. He promised to listen to the prayers of His children. "The LORD is far from the wicked, But He hears the prayer of the righteous" (Proverbs 15:29, NKJV).

Since the beginning of creation, God desired a relationship with mankind. The book of Genesis gives account of how God visited Adam and Eve every day to talk and spend time with them. They had a perfect relationship. However, when Adam and Eve disobeyed God, their sin destroyed that perfect relationship. Since the fall of mankind, Sin became a barrier between us and God (Isaiah 59:1-

2). Nevertheless, God loved us so much that He created a way to restore our relationship with Him. He gave us Jesus, the bridge between us and God. "For God so loved the world that He gave His only begotten Son, that whoever believes in Him should not perish but have everlasting life" (John 3:16, NKJV).

Today, He is still looking to build that same relationship with you. You do not need to hide anything from Him. He is willing to accept you because He loves you. There is nothing that can separate God's love from you. "For I am persuaded that neither death nor life, nor angels nor principalities nor powers, nor things present nor things to come, nor height nor depth, nor any other created thing, shall be able to separate us from the love of God which is in Christ Jesus our Lord" (Romans 8:38-39).

We wrote this book because we believe in prayer. The power of prayer changed our lives and strengthens our relationship with God. We believe that it will change your life as well. We hope you read this book as often as possible. We also pray that you practice what you learn from this book and share the principles with someone else. This book will teach you how to talk to God effectively. As you continue to talk to God, and read and apply His word, you will develop an intimate relationship with Him. That is the ultimate purpose of this guide to prayer. In this powerful book, you will learn the following:

1. **What is Prayer?**
2. **The Purpose of Prayer**
3. **The Power of Prayer**
4. **The Lord's Prayer**
5. **The 3 Keys to Effective Prayer**
6. **Top 20 prayers of all time**

Chapter 1

WHAT IS PRAYER?

"Prayer is a discipline that when exercised will give you a greater intimacy with your heavenly Father, but when neglected will make you feel distanced from Him" (Kay Arthur).

Prayer is a vital subject in spiritual health. The words prayer, pray and praying are mentioned over 500 times in the King James Version of the Holy Bible. It is obvious that God has a lot to say about prayer. Since it is important to God, it should be important to His children.

The Bible records many stories that teach us the importance of prayer. God wants us to pray, because He wants to develop relationship with us. Therefore, it is important to understand the meaning of prayer.

Some people would agree that they do not know the first thing about prayer. This is often true for many new Christians. Most of us were introduced to prayer in a church service. I remember the first time I heard someone pray. It was in my old church during a Sunday night service. Back then, it was called evangelizing service; but we never had any new converts. It was always the same people. At the beginning of the service, the pastor would ask Sister Marie, an Elder, to pray to invite the Holy Spirit into the service. As a child, I always wondered why the Holy Spirit had to be invited to every service. Why did he keep leaving?

Sister Marie's prayers were always fun to listen to, although I never really understood what she said. Though I would occasionally make out some of the words, I always got lost in the "thous" and "thuses". Furthermore, her prayers were always long and loud. As a kid, I always wondered if God was deaf, because in my church, prayer was **loud**! The louder it was, the better everybody felt.

I know that this is a comedic view of my introduction to prayer, but I am sure some of you can relate to it. Prayer does not have to be complicated or intimidating. However, it must be a vital part of everyday life. When it comes to the subject of prayer, it is always best to keep it simple. *"Simplicity is the Glory of expression"* (Walt Whitman).

Prayer is important because it is powerful and it changes lives. It is a form of communication with God. When we pray effectively, we express our thoughts, feelings and behaviors to Him. ***Prayer is the pipeline between us and our maker.*** We were created by God to be in a relationship with Him. Prayer is the means by which we build that relationship. ***Prayer is a heartfelt expression***

between two beings. It is an honest conversation between you and God.

The key to effective prayer is honesty. Honesty means to be sincere in expressing your emotions, thoughts and behaviors. It is not enough to just say empty words; your heart must be involved. *"When you pray, don't babble on and on as people of other religions do. They think their prayers are answered merely by repeating their words again and again. Don't be like them, for your Father knows exactly what you need even before you ask him!"* (Matthew 6:7-9, NLT).

Here are a few synonyms for prayer: appeal, plea, request, desire and hope. **Prayer expresses the desires of our hearts to whom we pray.** It is a heartfelt expression of desire that builds a strong bond with God. God wants us to pray to Him as much as we can. The more you talk to God and read about Him, the more you get to know Him. The same is true for your best friend or your Hero.

Prayer can be vertical or horizontal. We pray to each other as much as we pray to God. When you tell your loved ones what you desire for your birthday or for Christmas, you are making a request. This request is an expression of your heart and it is similar to prayer. Praying to God is very similar to making a request to your loved ones. When you pray to God, act like a child making a Christmas list; do not be afraid to ask for anything.

Prayer is not complicated; it is as simple as a son expressing his heart's desire to his dad. That kind of heartfelt expression is vital to building a strong bond between father and child. God wants to know you and give you what your heart desires. *"Delight yourself in the Lord and He will give you the desires of your heart"* (Psalm 37:4, NIV). God is the greatest giver in the universe. **He loves to give.** He has so much in store for you and He cannot wait to shower you with His blessings. All you have to do is ask. It is just that simple.

Now this is the confidence that we have in Him, that if we ask anything according to His will, He hears us. And if we know that He hears us, whatever we ask, we know that we have the petitions that we have asked of Him (1 John 5:14-15, NKJV).

Therefore I say to you, whatever things you ask when you pray, believe that you receive them, and you will have them (Mark 11:24, NKJV).

Maybe you are wondering if this is true. Will God really give you the desires of your heart? What if you desire something bad? It does not matter, since God will always answer with what is **best** for **you**. For example, if your child made some wrong choices in their life and is not sure how to fix the situation. Who would you want her to talk to? Most of us would prefer that our child talk to us rather than their peers or a stranger. Even if the child is afraid and ashamed, a loving parent will always lead the child in the right direction, through love.

It is the same way with God. *"If you abide in Me, and My words abide in you, you will ask what you desire, and it shall be done for you"* (John 15:07, NKJV). To God, your honesty is more important than your situation. It is always best to express your true desire to God, regardless of what others may think about your request. God will give you what you **need**. If you need to be redirected, He will gently show you the right way. He always answers with the truth. As promised, God will lead us into all truth and His truth will make us free. He always keeps His promises. Therefore, if we trust Him, He will lead us to the right path of life. As He leads us to the truth, we will find the desires of our hearts and true freedom. If we want to live according to God's truth, we must continue to believe in Him. Let us reflect on these scriptures:

However, when He, the Spirit of truth, has come, He will guide you into all truth; for He will not speak on His own authority, but whatever He hears He will speak; and He will tell you things to come (John 16:13, NKJV).

And you shall know the truth, and the truth shall make you free (John 8:32, NKJV).

We want to share with you the following revelation. It deals with the meaning of prayer. One day while my wife was praying, God spoke to her and she wrote down these statements as she heard them:

What I intended prayer to be was an expression of desire. Faith is the result of desire, for hope is anticipated fulfillment of desire. Your desire is what you long for, what or whom you long to be with. Your desire is where your heart is. Your desire is your greatest treasure and will be your greatest reward. It is where you place your faith, hope and love. Unfulfilled desire makes the heart sick while fulfilled desire brings life.

Prayer makes it possible for us to express our hearts desires to God. This kind of expression is based on love, faith and wisdom. This kind of prayer will build the relationship that God desires with His children. God is ready to empower His children to achieve their hearts' desires. He wants them to live according to the purpose He designed for them.

Prayer enables us to build an intimate relationship with our Heavenly Father, and that is the most important relationship of all. All relationships have some value. However, your relationship with God is the most important. The relationships with friends, family and others are temporary, but your relationship with God is eternal. We were created to be in relationship with God. The desire to be connected to your maker is the deepest need of the human soul.

This desire is due to the fact that we were created in God's image and likeness (Genesis 1:26). Many have expressed emptiness in their souls that nothing else could satisfy until they got connected to God. There is a place in your soul that only a loving God can fill. Nothing in this world can satisfy that need, only the love of God can give you complete fulfillment. There are good things in this world that give some fulfillment, however they are temporary. Only God's love lasts forever, that is why prayer is so important. As you continue to pray and grow in your relationship with God, your life will be transformed.

Chapter 2

THE PURPOSE OF PRAYER

Prayer does not change the purpose of God. But prayer does change the action of God" (Chuck Smith).

People pray for various reasons and pack God's "prayer inbox" with innumerable requests. When I wonder how God keeps up with all the requests, it often reminds me of a scene in the movie "Bruce Almighty" where Jim Carey's character resorts to using a laptop in an effort to keep up with all of the prayer requests. Despite all the available technology, he was not even able to answer a mere fraction of the incoming prayer requests. In this chapter, let's focus on why we pray, why we experience difficult times and how to exercise prayer in difficult times.

The primary reason for prayer is to establish a personal relationship with our Heavenly Father. Prayer should not be used simply to request things from God. Rather, it should be used to strengthen the bond you have with God. When you have a strong bond with God, you can boldly come before Him with any request, and you know without the shadow of a doubt that He will always give you what is best. However, when prayer is used simply as a means to get what you want, you fail to develop trust.

God is Omniscient and Omnipotent, meaning He is all Knowing and all Powerful. When you make requests before Him, He chooses how He wants to respond; and sometimes His response appears peculiar. God is also Sovereign, which means He is Supreme. He cannot be controlled nor will He be manipulated. Therefore, it is best to pray earnestly and give Him the freedom to choose how and when He will answer your prayers. God is love, and as we learn to accept and receive His love, we will trust Him with our deepest desires.

Second, we pray for things we desire; for it is our desires that lead us to pray with passion. This passionate prayer is called "Fervent Prayer." In the New Living Translation (NTL) Bible, it is called "Earnest Prayer." It is that honest plea that touches the heart of God. It is bold, loving and without fear. God said that He found in King David a man according to His own heart. We believe that David's honesty before God is one of the main reasons for such an honorable claim. Remember this truth when praying: Prayer is relational and should be guided by love. *"There is no fear in love; but perfect love casts out fear, because fear involves torment. But he who fears has not been made perfect in love"* (1 John 4:18, NKJV).

Keep in mind that kind of fear creates barriers in relationships. Therefore, when you pray you must do so in love. **Open your heart and be bare before God.** Do not be afraid to say anything you want, since nothing can take God's love away from you.

Thirdly, we pray to God because we are His sons and daughters. He created us in His image and likeness. He redeemed us from sin and death. He made us heirs of His kingdom. *"Therefore you are no longer a slave but a son, and if a son, then an heir of God through Christ"* (Galatians 4:7, NKJV).

Pray to your Heavenly Father to strengthen your relationship with Him. You need an open line of communication for open access to all the resources available to you as His Child.

Now, imagine that your father is a billionaire, but you have no contact with him. How can you ever have access to his riches? Building a healthy relationship with your Heavenly Father will keep you close to His heart, and thus grant you full access to his blessings. Although God is faithful to keep His promises, we often make His job difficult when we disobey His commandments. When we disobey, we often experience negative consequences.

Why we experience difficult times

People often pray more during difficult times. We believe that it's a great idea! When praying during difficult times, it is important to remember that God loves YOU! The problems of this world are not God's will. God is not the enemy, but your friend. He wants the best for you, because He loves you. Knowing this fact will help you with the challenges of your life.

God is often blamed for the many problems of life. However, He is not always the driving force. After all, He created the universe in perfection. The earth and everything in it was perfect until the fall of mankind as influenced by the devil. When you pray for solutions to life's difficulties, it is important to understand the root cause of these problems. This will help you to remain focused on the solution that you seek. It will help you not to blame God or others for the challenges of life. Obviously, we cannot fully describe life's problems in a single book. However, we want to examine some of the reasons why we face problems in this life.

The primary reason is the fall of mankind. We lost perfection when Adam and Eve disobeyed God. You can read the Biblical account of the fall of mankind in the book of Genesis 3:1-24. Since we are living in an imperfect world with imperfect people, we often experience negative outcomes. We cannot control life; we do not have that power.

We cannot prevent natural disasters nor can we stop tragedy. However, we can pray. We can pray for God's will to be done on earth as it is in heaven.

Prayer can superimpose the power of nature when fueled by faith and passion. We will face difficulties in this imperfect world we live in; however, prayer can help us overcome. "I have told you these things, so that in me you may have peace. In this world you will have trouble. But take heart! I have overcome the world" (John 16:33, NIV).

The next reason we face challenges in life is because we have an enemy. His name is Satan. His mission is to attempt to steal everything that God has for His children, to kill and to destroy God's creation (John 10:10). But we find hope in knowing that *"... When the enemy comes in like a flood, the Spirit of the LORD will lift up a standard against him"* (Isaiah 59:19, NKJV).

The devil accomplishes his mission by influencing people to do his will. The devil works diligently to persuade people to fulfill his wishes. He studies our weaknesses and he understands how our mindset affects our behavior. As a result, he knows exactly how to influence our choices.

The battle begins in the mind, because the Bible tells us that we become what we think or meditate on. *"For as he thinks in his heart, so is he..."* (Proverbs 3:27a). Make no mistakes: the devil hates us and will stop at nothing to destroy us and our loved ones. But we do not have to be afraid of the devil, because Jesus was sent to earth so that we may have life and have it more abundantly. To achieve this mission, Jesus destroyed the works of the devil at the cross. *"...For this purpose the Son of God was manifested, that He might destroy the works of the devil"* (1 John 3:8b).

Furthermore, Jesus gave us power over the forces of darkness. *"Behold, I give you the authority to trample on serpents and scorpions, and over all the power of the enemy, and nothing shall by any means hurt you"* (Luc 19:19,NKJV). We know that the enemy will attack us. However, we should not be afraid, because with prayer we can tap into God's power to defeat Satan.

Our poor decisions and the decisions of others are the third reason we experience difficulties in this life. The outcomes of life can be positive as we make positive choices, or negative as we make negative choices. We are all faced with choices every day, and every choice we make will have consequences. But the decisions of *others* can *also* impact our lives. Imperfect people will make imperfect decisions, and others will be victimized as a result.

For example, if a mother abuses drugs and alcohol while pregnant, that child is more likely to have birth defects. Here is another example: If parents do not learn how to manage their personal finances, they will have fewer resources to effectively raise their children.

We must be responsible for our actions, and learn from our mistakes. If we do not, we will continue to make the same errors. History has proved that if we do not learn any lesson from the past, we are more likely to repeat it. We must stop blaming God and the devil, and start being responsible.

The answers to most of our problems begin by looking within. We must not blame God for the consequences of our bad choices. Instead, we must repent and seek His loving grace. *"Do not be deceived, God is not mocked; for whatever a man sows, that he will also reap. For he who sows to his flesh will of the flesh reap corruption, but he who sows to the Spirit will of the Spirit reap everlasting life"* (Galatians 6:7-8, NKJV). We cannot control what others do; we can only control what *we* do. Since we are imperfect we all will make bad decisions at one point or another during our lifetime. However, with God we can overcome any situation, no matter the outcome.

We are all familiar with the saying, "what goes around comes around." The principle behind this saying is found in the Bible. The lesson we should learn from that principle is the following: what we give out will eventually come back to us. This is true whether we sow good or bad seeds. We will reap what we have sown. If we make wise decisions today, we will have a better tomorrow. If you lack wisdom—which most of us do—the Bible tells us that we can ask God for wisdom. *"If any of you lacks wisdom, let him ask of God, who gives to all liberally and without reproach, and it will be given to him"* (James 1:5, NKJV). As we apply wisdom, we will make better choices and will be blessed with a much happier life.

Wisdom helps us become more responsible for our lives. While we have no power over others, God gave us power over our own lives. He has given us the power to produce our hearts' desires. He gave us the power of choice. We can choose to live our lives according to His will, or according to our own sinful desires. If we live according to God's will, we will have eternal life. It is up to us to apply God's principles to succeed in life. If you are struggling in life, we recommend that you reflect on these questions: "Why am I struggling, and what is stopping me from being successful in life?" As you ponder these questions, you can also ask God to reveal the truth to you and send you people to help you. God will do what you cannot do. However, He expects you to practice your faith and produce what you can with the current strengths and resources you have. As you apply the wisdom found in God's word, you will be empowered to make better choices in life.

In life, we all will have different hurdles to jump over as we move toward the finish line. Some of them will be higher and others will be lower. The way we handle life's hurdles will determine how quickly we get to the finish line, and whether we win or lose the race. Let's look closely at some of the things we can do to better manage life's difficulties.

How to exercise prayer in difficult times

When life gets difficult, we should first and foremost pray, pray and pray. Prayer has proven to be effective for God's children for many centuries, and you are invited to try it. Remember, prayer has the power to reduce harmful stress. We know that the less harmful stress we have, the better our life will be. Our minds will be clearer to face life difficulties when there is less stress.

The truth is that we are all subject to the problems and realities of life. We are all dealt with different *cards of life*. For many, it is not the king, the queen or the ace. It is the unexpected children with a disability. For others, it is a broken home, blindness, the loss of a loved one or the cancer diagnosis at twenty-six years old. These are some of the cards people are dealing with.

It does not matter if you are a Christian, a Jew, a Muslim or an Atheist; we all have to face the reality of life. There is no easy way to play the cards we were dealt with by life. We must play them day by day.

Prayer helps us bring the focus on the solution rather than the problems of life. As we pray, we will be able to partner with God and use his power to overcome our troubles. The way we handle our problems determines our quality of life. As we continue to express our hearts in prayer, we will maintain a positive attitude. Prayer is essential to prevail in life.

King David found prayer to be beneficial when he was in trouble. We have outlined two of his most quoted prayers below. As you meditate on these prayers, let their messages bring hope and peace to your heart.

The LORD is my shepherd; I shall not want. He makes me to lie down in green pastures; He leads me beside the still waters. He restores my soul; He leads me in the paths of righteousness For His name's sake. Yea, though I walk through the valley of the shadow of death, I will fear no evil; for you are with me; your rod and your staff, they comfort me. You prepare a table before me in the presence of my enemies; you anoint my head with oil; my cup runs over. Surely goodness and mercy shall follow me all the days of my life; and I will dwell in the house of the LORD Forever (Psalm 23:1-6, NKJV).

Those who live in the shelter of the Most High will find rest in the shadow of the Almighty. This I declare about the LORD: He alone is my refuge, my place of safety; He is my God, and I trust Him. For He will rescue you from every trap and protect you from deadly disease. He will cover you with His feathers. He will shelter you with His wings. His faithful promises are your armor and protection. Do not be afraid of the terrors of the night, nor the arrow that flies in the day. Do not dread the disease that stalks in darkness, nor the disaster that strikes at midday. Though a thousand fall at your side, though ten thousand are dying around you, these evils will not touch you. Just open your eyes, and see how the wicked are punished (Psalm 91:1-8, NLT).

We should also pray to God and ask him to bring loving people to help us in difficult times. We should seek help and support from others when facing those difficult times in life. The journey of life was not meant to be taken alone. God declared, *"It is not good that man should be alone; I will make him a helper comparable to him"* (Genesis 2:18, NKJV). We should seek God's help and the help from loving people when we are in trouble.

This world can be cold, especially if you do not have someone to warm you up along the way. When life brings hardship and unexpected problems, you can choose to believe in God who is higher than any problems of life. We urge you to seek guidance from God and from others. Life is too complex to undertake alone. We all need help from others in life.

Even God collaborated with people to achieve greatness on earth. For example, he partnered with Mary to give birth to the Messiah, Jesus. If you are willing, He can partner with *you* as well. The bible encourages a team approach to life. If you are not using a team approach, your success in life will be limited. The word of God declares *"Confess your sins to each other and pray for each other so that you may be healed"* (James 5:16, NLT).

It is important to pray for each other because *"The earnest prayer of a righteous person has great power and produces wonderful results"* (James 5:16, NLT). Furthermore, there is greater power in numbers. Jesus declared, *"I also tell you this: If two of you agree here on earth concerning anything you ask, my Father in heaven will do it for you"* (Matthew 18:19, NLT).

Acquiring the support of others is essential because our enemy the devil preys on easy targets: those who are weak and isolated. The word of God warns us to "*Stay alert! Watch out for your great enemy, the devil. He prowls around like a roaring lion, looking for someone to devour*" (1 Peter, 5:8). It is more difficult for a lion to catch potential prey that is in a group, because the prey has the protection of the group. There is power in numbers. When we seek the help and support of others in the journey of life, we will have increased strength and power to triumph in that journey.

Furthermore, it is vital to pray for increased faith in the promises of God during difficult times. Faith in the word of God is the catalyst to our victory. If you believe, you will receive. God has the power to protect His children. He has the power to protect *you* from the storms of life and from the enemy.

God protected Daniel when he was thrown in the lion's den, and He can do the same for you. *"The LORD Himself goes before you and will be with you; He will never leave you nor forsake you. Do not be afraid; do not be discouraged"* (Deuteronomy 31:8, NIV). *"The LORD will not forsake His people, for His great name's sake, because it has pleased the*

LORD to make you His people" (1 Samuel 12:22, NKJV).

Jesus also left us a very comforting promise to help in difficult times. We hope that you find His statements inspiring and comforting. *"I have told you these things, so that in me you may have peace. In this world you will have trouble. But take heart! I have overcome the world."* (John 16:33, NIV). *"Peace I leave with you; my peace I give you. I do not give to you as the world gives. Do not let your hearts be troubled and do not be afraid"* (John 14:27, NIV).

Since our Lord overcame this world, we will also overcome it. In Christ, we are **victors** and not *victims* of this world. Therefore, we challenge you to rise above the storms of life, through faith. God will empower you to soar like an eagle above the storm. The essential step to rise above your problems is that you must believe. If you believe you can fly, it will come to pass.

God will never abandon you, for He loves you. No matter what you are facing, keep in mind that it will not last forever. After the night, daybreak will always come. Today's problems cannot stop tomorrow from coming. If you are going through a difficult time as you read this, call on God for help, and surround yourself with loving people for support and guidance. Again, you can be assured of these three principles:

1. *With God all things are possible.*
2. *Your problems will not last forever, and you will overcome your problems as you put your trust in God.*
3. *God will never forsake you.*

We pray that you find God's word comforting, and let His truth encourage you to face everyday life. He promised His children a life companion who will never forsake us. This is from the Lord Jesus Christ, *"The Counselor, the Holy Spirit, whom the Father will send in my name, will teach you all things and will remind you of everything I have said to you." When He, the Spirit of truth, comes, He will guide you into all truth. He will not speak on His own; He will speak only what He hears, and He will tell you what is yet to come"* (John 14:26 & John 16:13, NIV).

Moreover, when praying in difficult times it is important to be persistent. Persistence will keep you focused on the desired outcome. We recommend that you stand on God's word, for it is **powerful!** It continues to be the main instrument in our life success. If you stand on the Word of God and act accordingly, you will be empowered to overcome the crisis of life. As mentioned, if you do not quit in life, you will eventually win. We find truth in the statement: "a quitter never wins, and a winner never quits." We pray that you will meditate on this principle. *"God will bless you, if you don't give up when your faith is being tested. He will reward you with a glorious life, [a] just as he rewards everyone who loves him"* (James 1:12, CEV).

Finally, to overcome in difficult times, it's important to surrender to the Lordship of Christ. Pray that your heart will hearken to God's purpose for your life. Life is like a thrilling novel, and *you* are the main character. Every day a new page is written in this great story...about *you*! The book was created by the author of life, however, He allows us to choose every day whether we want to write our own story, or let *Him* do it. My friend, I do not have to tell you how much better your novel will be if the **Author of Life** is given the opportunity to carve it!

When you allow God to write your story, you find your purpose, because surrender **always** leads to purpose. "A life without purpose is a meaningless life" (James Justin). A life without purpose is like driving a car in the dark with no functioning brakes or headlights. Since God is the creator, only He knows why He created you and His purpose for your life.

Sometimes difficulties arise when we are living outside of God's purpose for our lives; that is why it is important to surrender to his guidance and will for your life. We all need to know our purpose here on earth, and the Heavenly Father is the only one who knows what that purpose is. He is the one we must go to in order to discover our life's purpose.

You can read as many self-help books, psychological books and other books to find your life purpose, but no one can do it better than the inventor of life. There is nothing wrong with reading these books, but keep in mind that God is the best source, since He created you. As you continue praying, reading God's word and letting Him write your life story, He will guide you into your destiny. It will be the best novel you have ever read!

Prayer should not be passive, but should be proactive. In relationships, both parties should be involved. When you pray, you have *your* part to play. For example, if you are praying for a job, act on faith and start sending out résumés and apply where there is a job opening. It is not enough to just ask God for a job; you must also do your part. It is important to remember that God is not a magician, He is a Father. He empowers His children by encouraging them to perform activities that they can do on their own.

God will perform things for us that require divine intervention. For example, Moses could not separate the Red Sea with his own human power, but he *could* raise his staff and stretch out his hand over the sea as instructed by God. As Moses did his part, God separated the sea. You can read this powerful story in Exodus 14:1-31.

God wants His children to grow and become mature. He will fulfill His responsibilities as a Father; He will provide, protect, save, lead, instruct and love. Likewise, He expects His children to fulfill *their* responsibilities, such as obey His word, respond to His love and talk to Him. As you do your part and let God do His part, you will develop a stronger relationship with your Heavenly Father and have a more meaningful life on earth.

We cannot imagine our lives without prayer, for it is as important to us as breathing. Prayer has drastically changed our lives, and we believe it will change *yours* as well. We urge you to include prayer in your daily life. Since God is not a respecter of persons, He will answer your prayers as well. If you call on God, He will answer you. In prayer, you can knock at God's door, and He will open it. If you seek Him diligently, you will find Him. In fact, God is closer than you may think.

Some religions teach that God can only be found in the heavens. This means that one must reach some spiritual height before finding Him. However, God made it easier for us. He came down to us through His Son, Jesus Christ. Jesus became the portal for us to connect to God. Therefore, we do not need to wait until we reach a certain spiritual height; we can pray to God directly.

As your Father, He dwells in you through the Holy Spirit. You don't need to search very far. If you need to talk, He is available to listen at all times. If you need a blessing, you can ask Him today...or right now. He is ready to bless you. In fact, there are over 7,000 blessings recorded in the Bible. As you pray to God, be bold and be passionate, for everything you need is already stored up for you.

There are many reasons why people pray. We pray first and foremost to establish an intimate relationship with God. We pray for things we desire. We pray because we are God's sons and daughters. Lastly, we pray for help in difficult times. Prayer is fundamental to our very survival in this world we live in. However, as much as it is important to understand the purpose of prayer, it is also very important to understand *how* to pray. In the next chapter, we reveal the steps for effective prayer according to the guide Jesus taught his disciples.

Chapter 3

THE POWER OF PRAYER

In 1970, the Classic Soul Legend Aretha Franklin wrote and performed the hit song, "I Say A Little Prayer." This song inspired so many people throughout the world. The song was so powerful that it even influenced some scientists to investigate the benefits of prayer.

Dr. William Harris was one of the scientists who studied the benefits of prayer. He conducted his initial study from St. Luke's Hospital, Kansas City, Missouri. The results of his study revealed that prayer made a difference in the recovery process of patients. The patients who received prayer recovered quicker and had fewer hospital stays than those who did not receive any prayer.

The St. Luke's Study was conducted with patients who were being treated for cardiac problems. This research study was an attempt to replicate the 1988 study on intercessory prayer conducted at San Francisco General Hospital. Both studies revealed that prayer played a positive impact in the healing process. These research studies show the benefit of prayer. They revealed that prayer in combination with medical science helped in the healing process of the patients involved. You can read the details on the St. Luke's study in the October 25, 1999 issue of the *Archives of Internal Medicine*.

If prayer worked for the patients in the research studies mentioned, we believe it will work for you as well. Prayer has the power to heal your physical, psychological and spiritual conditions. **This chapter examines the Biblical perspective on the power of prayer; 10 benefits of prayer; spiritual warfare; intercessory prayer and fasting.**

Although medical science has shed some light on the benefits of prayer; we believe that the Bible is the primary source to understand prayer. This is because prayer involves faith. Those who pray must believe in it. We believe that the power of prayer comes from God and not from the person who prays. Without God's power, prayer is as powerless and meaningless as the unsalted salt.

As you explore the power of prayer and its benefits, you may first want to develop your faith in God and in prayer. What's faith? It is *"the substance of things hoped for, the evidence of things not seen"* (Hebrews 11:1). Faith is important because it is impossible to please God without first believe in Him.

As Christians, we believe that the answers to our prayers come from God. We believe that there is only one God, and Jesus Christ is the way to Him. This is what Jesus says, *"I am the way, the truth, and the life. No one comes to the Father except through me"* (John 14:6, NKJV). Since faith is so important in prayer, we cannot rely on science alone to help us understand the subject of prayer.

Power of Prayer based on the Bible

The Bible records several accounts describing the power of prayer. We have highlighted just a few in this chapter. The power of prayer has overcome enemies (Psalm 6:9-10), conquered death (2 Kings 4:3-36), brought healing (James 5:14-15) and defeated demons (Mark 9:29). God, through prayer, opens eyes, changes hearts, heals wounds and grants wisdom (James 1:5).

The Bible also declares, *"Confess your trespasses to one another, and pray for one another, that you may be healed. The effective, fervent prayer of a righteous man avails much. Elijah was a man with a nature like ours and he prayed earnestly that it would not rain; and it did not rain on the land for three years and six months. And he prayed again, and the heaven gave rain, and the earth produced its fruit"* (James 5:16-18, NKJV). Now, that's powerful!

10 Benefits of Prayer

The benefits of prayer are too enormous to list. We mentioned some of the benefits of prayer throughout this book. However, we want to highlight 10 powerful benefits. These benefits can be experienced as we continue to practice the principle of effective prayer. Here are 10 benefits of prayer:

1. Prayer will help you maintain a healthy lifestyle by reducing harmful stress. In prayer, you'll develop closer relationship with God; find inner peace and relaxation which are needed to boost your immune system to fight inflammations and some diseases.
2. Prayer can create a peaceful and relaxing atmosphere (1Timothy 2:1).
3. Prayer can help you forgive others and yourself (1 John 1:9).
4. Prayer keeps one from entering into temptation: Jesus told His disciples in the garden to watch and pray that they may not fall into temptation and sin.
5. Prayer causes the heavens to open: Jesus prayed and the heaven was opened (Luke 3:21).
6. Prayer prepares one for the Holy Spirit to come: When Jesus prayed the heaven was

opened and the Holy Spirit descended in a bodily shape like a dove upon him (Luke 3:22).

7. Prayer positions one to hear God speak: The Bible declares that a voice came from heaven which said, "thou art my beloved Son in thee I am well pleased" (Luke 3:22).
8. Prayer can deliver you from danger: Daniel prayed three times a day and was delivered from the lion's den.
9. Prayer brings boldness to share the Gospel (Acts 4:23).
10. Prayer builds one up spiritually (Jude 1:20).

You can now enjoy the benefits of prayer and release the power of God over your life by developing a personal relationship with God. The closer you get to God, the more you will know Him and His ways. If you draw near to Him, He will draw near to you (James 4:8).

The power of prayer is not released by the person who prays, rather it is from God. Since God listens to His children, you can be sure that your prayer will activate God's Divine Power to transform your life. We recommend that you pray from your heart, have a clear purpose and pray according to God's word. God answers prayers that are in agreement with His will and promises. His answers are not always yes, but they are always in our best interest. He is a father and He knows what is best for His children.

As you grow and develop in your relationship with God through prayer, you will strengthen your commitment to Him. You will become more honest and you will establish an incredible amount of trust in the relationship. This will create a strong foundation and will allow you to delve further into deeper realms of prayer with unmatched confidence.

There are certain challenges you encounter in life that requires deeper realms of prayer. For example, in the case of the little boy who was under the control of the deaf and dumb evil spirit, Jesus told the disciples, *"This kind cannot be driven out by anything but prayer and fasting"* (Mark 9:29, AMP). In this particular case, fasting was an additional necessity to resolve the situation. Fasting is different than prayer in that you can pray without fasting or vice versa. We'll further discuss prayer later.

There are certain situations in our lives that will require more than just prayer. Up until this point, we have only focused on prayer directed toward God. However, prayer can be used against the kingdom of darkness in what we Christians call spiritual warfare. For the remainder of this chapter, we will give you a brief overview on the subject of spiritual warfare, intercessory prayer and fasting.

Spiritual Warfare

Spiritual warfare plays a vital part of Christian development. This concept is well recorded in the book of Ephesians chapter six:

Finally, be strong in the Lord and in His mighty power. Put on the full armor of God so that you can take your stand against the devil's schemes. For our struggle is not against flesh and blood, but against the rulers, against the authorities, against the powers of this dark world and against the spiritual forces of evil in the heavenly realms. Therefore put on the full armor of God, so that when the day of evil comes, you may be able to stand your ground, and after you have done everything, to stand. Stand firm then, with the belt of truth buckled around your waist, with the breastplate of righteousness in place, and with your feet fitted with the readiness that comes from the gospel of peace. In addition to all this, take up the shield of faith, with which you can extinguish all the flaming arrows of the evil one. Take the helmet of salvation and the sword of the Spirit, which is the word of God. And pray in the Spirit on all occasions with all kinds of prayers and requests. With this in mind, be alert and always keep on praying for all the saints (Ephesians 6:10-18, NIV).

Spiritual warfare is a vast topic and deserves its own book. However, we will give you a brief overview, for no book on prayer is complete without a discussion on spiritual warfare. For simplicity, we define spiritual warfare as the battle between the children of God and the devil. The mission of the devil is to steal, kill and destroy, but Jesus' mission is to give us life and life more abundantly (John 10:10).

Also, Jesus came to destroy the devil's work in our lives. *"...The reason the Son of God appeared was to destroy the devil's work"* (1 John 3:8, NIV). This spiritual war is waged in the spirit, but it can affect the soul and the body. It affects the systems of this world. As human beings, we are influenced by the force of good and evil. As soon as we are conceived, we are automatically drafted in the battle between good and evil—this is what we call spiritual warfare. We are born in this war because we are born in sin. King David said it this way, *"Surely I was sinful at birth, sinful from the time my mother conceived me"* (Psalms 51:5, NKJV). Spiritual warfare is real. We all face it on a daily basis. We face it in the choices we make and in the activities we engage in. We constantly have to choose between the force of good and evil, and this is spiritual warfare.

The Bible is the only weapon you need in this fight. The Apostle Paul explains, *"The weapons we fight with are not the weapons of the world. On the contrary, they have divine power to demolish strongholds. We demolish arguments and every pretension that sets itself up against the knowledge of God, and we take captive every thought to make it obedient to Christ"* (2 Corinthians 10:4-5, NIV).

God created us with free will; as a result we decide whose kingdom will reign over our lives through the thoughts we entertain and the choices we make. If we live according to our sinful desires and the force of evil, we will lose the battle and never connect with our Heavenly father. However, if we live according to the will of God, eternal life awaits us. *"For if you live according to [the dictates of] the flesh, you will surely die. But if through the power of the [Holy] Spirit you are [habitually] putting to death (making extinct, deadening) the [evil] deeds prompted by the body, you shall [really and genuinely] live forever"* (Romans 8:13, AMP). As you build an intimate relationship with God, He will empower you to live according to His standard and become a winner in this spiritual warfare.

In the Lord's Prayer, Jesus encourages us to pray for God's will to be done on Earth as it is in heaven. It would be easy to have God's will be done all the time, if we did not have an enemy. However, we have an enemy whose goal is to steal all God's blessings away from us, and attempt to kill and destroy all God's children. You do not have to be afraid because Jesus won the war so that you can walk in victory as you continue to obey Him. Jesus said, *"For my Father has given them to me, and he is more powerful than anyone else. No one can snatch them from the Father's hand"* (John 10:29, NLT).

You can never lose when you make Jesus your Lord, Savior and friend. How do you win in spiritual warfare? You must submit to God and resist the devil and he will flee from you (James 4:7). The Bible also teaches us to be alert and watch out for the enemy. *"Stay alert! Watch out for your great enemy, the devil. He prowls around like a roaring lion, looking for someone to devour. Stand firm against him, and be strong in your faith"* (1 Peter 5:8-9a, NLT). There are many different ways you can engage in spiritual warfare, for simplicity's sake we will only discuss two methods, Intercession and Fasting.

Intercessory Prayer

Intercessory Prayer is the process of praying on behalf of yourself and others. An intercessor is one who takes the place of another or who pleads on behalf of another's case. It is like a lawyer who represents his or her client's case. For instance, you may choose to pray for the salvation of a loved one. When you intercede for them, your prayer will act as a shield to protect them until they make the decision for Christ. Another great case for intercessory prayer is where a father prays for blessings for his children and spouse.

For Christians, Jesus Christ is our model for Intercessory Prayer, and He is the great intercessor. He stands before God every day to intercede for us, just as the Old Testament priests prayed and ministered on behalf of the people of Israel. *"For there [is only] one God, and [only] one Mediator between God and men, the Man Christ Jesus, Who gave Himself as a ransom for all [people, a fact that was] attested to at the right and proper time"* (1Timothy 2:5-6, AMP).

Jesus is our intercessor, Lord and Savior. He died and rose again to pay the price of our sins and to redeem us from the consequences of sin. He conquered death so that we may have eternal life (John 10:10). Therefore He is able, once and forever, to save those who come to God through Him. He lives forever to intercede with God on our behalf (Hebrews 7:25). Jesus was an intercessor while He was here on earth. He prayed for those who were sick and possessed by demons. He prayed for His disciples. He even prayed for you and me when He interceded for all those who would believe in Him. Jesus continued His ministry of intercession after His death and resurrection when He returned to Heaven. He now serves as our intercessor in Heaven. Likewise, we are encouraged to stand in intercession for one another because lives depend on it.

Fasting

Fasting is another important aspect of the Christian life development. We like the way Dr. Dan B. Allender defines fasting in his book, ***The Wounded Heart***, "Fasting is the choice to put aside legitimate satisfaction, for a time, to concentrate on a more pressing spiritual pursuit." He further explains that abstaining from pleasure helps us diminish our dependence on temporal satisfaction while allowing us to pursue a higher call. Since this book is not about fasting, we will not go into details. While some use fasting as a tool for mental cleansing and for general health, it has great value in spiritual warfare. Fasting causes you to deny yourself of certain pleasures in order to focus on a desired outcome.

The length of time and the method of fasting depend on the individual and the cause. Daniel fasted for twenty-one days. He ate lightly and drank. Jesus fasted for forty days but did not eat or drink. They both had different purposes for their fasts. When fasting, ask God to inspire you on the appropriate method and timeframe for the fast. It is also important to consult your physician prior to engaging in a fast.

Some people pray when they fast, however prayer is not required when fasting. You can fast without praying even though some people prefer to pray and fast simultaneously. Fasting is really a powerful tool. Many great men and women of the Bible used fasting to tap into the supernatural powers of God to change impossible situations here on earth. One such example is found in the book of Esther.

There was a decree to kill all the Jews in the land. Esther, the queen, was also a Jew. She wanted to approach the king and discuss the issue but in those days the queen could only go to the king when summoned. Esther knew that if she went to see the king without being summoned she could be killed, so she declared a nationwide fast for all the Jews. *"Go, gather together all the Jews that are present in Shushan, and fast for me; and neither eat nor drink for three days, night or day. I also and my maids will fast as you do. Then I will go to the king, though it is against the law; and if I perish, I perish"* (Esther 4:16, NKJV).

In this thriller, fasting did work. Esther was not killed when she went to see the King. In the end of the story, the Jews were saved and the man who ordered the genocide was executed. In this story you can see how fasting saved Esther and the entire Jewish nation in that Land. It not only saved them but caused the destruction of their enemy. Fasting is powerful. If you have a situation that seems impossible, perhaps fasting may be just what the doctor ordered. Fasting is very important in spiritual warfare.

In this chapter, we provided a Biblical perspective on the benefit and power of prayer. We discussed concepts such as the healing power of prayer, spiritual warfare, intercessory prayer and fasting. While these concepts play a vital role on the power of prayer, the focus must always be on the source. God is the only source. You can tap on this power by going to the source. We pray that God will empower you to pray with power and grant you the desires of your heart.

Chapter 4

THE LORD'S PRAYER

This chapter will teach you how to pray effectively. The best pattern for effective prayer comes directly from the master Himself, Jesus Christ. He is the most qualified to teach on prayer, since He came from heaven and knows what moves God.

Jesus taught His disciples how to pray by giving them a simple guide to follow. This prayer is commonly known as the Lord's Prayer, and recorded in Matthew 6:9-13. As requested by the original 12 disciples, Jesus taught them how to pray. The motive of Jesus was simply to teach the *disciples* how to pray, but to this day *all* of God's people still follow the principles of this teaching. Since this great prayer gives us an outline on how to pray, let's examine it line by line and study the principles that are embedded in it.

"Our Father which art in heaven"

As a child of God, it's important to honor Him. We show honor to God by acknowledging who He is. We do so by highlighting and praising Him for who He is. He is our Heavenly Father. He is above all. He says *"I AM THAT I AM"* (Exodus 3:14, NKJV).

Address Him with respect, honor and reverence just as you would address your earthly father with respect.

Believe that He is the only God, who created all things in this universe. He created mankind in His own image and likeness (Genesis 1:26-31). He loves us and we need to show our love to Him. When we obey God's word we demonstrate our love for Him. God loves us so much that He gave His only Son, Jesus Christ, to die to redeem us from sin and death (John 3:16). This statement in the prayer identifies God as the Heavenly Father and us as His children. Therefore, we can come to Him without any fear.

"Hallowed be thy name"

This statement reflects God's sacredness. When we pray, we must acknowledge Him as He is. He is Holy, Sanctified, Consecrated, Honorable, full of Glory and Worthy of our praise! God wants His children to worship Him in spirit and in truth. It is His commandment that we worship Him only.

"Thy Kingdom come"

This is a simple act of surrendering our lives unto God. This statement requests for God's Kingdom to permeate ours. When we allow God to lead our lives, His Kingdom comes and it is a wonderful phenomenon. God's Kingdom is perfect, more powerful and more glorious then ours. It makes sense that we should submit our lives to His ruling. As you pray, open your heart to God; and His Kingdom will invade your life.

"Thy will be done on earth, as it is in heaven"

This line is simply explaining the previous statement in more detail. We should pray for His Will to be done in our lives, so that we might live according to His perfect will as it is in heaven. It is acceptable for us to tell God what our will is. However, we must place *His* Will above our own.

The will of God is perfect. Jesus demonstrated this in the Garden of Gethsemane when He was facing torture and death on the cross. It is written that Jesus fell on His face to the ground and prayed, *"O My Father, if it is possible, let this cup pass from Me; nevertheless, not as I will, but as You will"* (Matthew 26:39, NKJV). Again, as we continue to surrender our will to God's, our lives will blossom. The will of God is perfect and we need to pray that His will be done on earth as it is in heaven.

"Give us today our daily bread"

As we accept Jesus as our King, Lord and Savior, we acknowledge God as our provider. We must ask our Heavenly Father each day to provide for our needs. Again, God is willing to supply all of our needs in His perfect riches. *"And this same God who takes care of me will supply all your needs from his glorious riches, which have been given to us in Christ Jesus"* (Philippians 4:19, NLT). Jesus taught us to first seek God's will, and all of our earthly needs will be added unto us. *"Seek the Kingdom of God above all else, and live righteously, and he will give you everything you need"* (Matthew 6:33, NLT).

As God's children, we do not have to beg for anything. We have full access to our Father's riches. We simply need to ask God and apply His Words. God already promised to supply all our needs. Therefore, when praying for daily needs, pray with confidence that God will fulfill His promise. Keep in mind that He may surprise you. He may choose to respond to our requests in the least expected way. Why does He do that? We are not sure. He is Sovereign; therefore, He can do whatever He wants.

That is why I tell you not to worry about everyday life—whether you have enough food and drink, or enough clothes to wear. Isn't life more than food, and your body more than clothing? Look at the birds. They don't plant or harvest or store food in barns, for your heavenly Father feeds them. And aren't you far more valuable to him than they are? Can all your worries add a single moment to your life?

"And why worry about your clothing? Look at the lilies of the field and how they grow. They don't work or make their clothing, yet Solomon in all his glory was not dressed as beautifully as they are. And if God cares so wonderfully for wildflowers that are here today and thrown into the fire tomorrow, he will certainly care for you. Why do you have so little faith?

"So don't worry about these things, saying, 'What will we eat? What will we drink? What will we wear?' These things dominate the thoughts of unbelievers, but your heavenly Father already knows all your needs. Seek the Kingdom of God above all else, and live righteously, and he will give you everything you need (Matthew 6:25-33, NLT).

"Forgive us our debts (or transgressions) as we have forgiven our debtors"

What is forgiveness? It is an act of releasing a debt owed by another. Forgiveness is a hard choice. It requires God's love and human courage. Love is the only motivation for forgiveness. *Love keeps no record of wrong* (1 Corinthians 13:5). Why forgive? It is beneficial to our spirit, soul and body. When we forgive, we will be free of the burden of un-forgiveness and bitterness. *"To forgive is to set a prisoner free and discover that the prisoner was you"* (Lewis B. Smedes).

We also forgive because it is a commandment of God. He commands us to forgive those who transgress against us. *"Judge not, and you shall not be judged. Condemn not, and you shall not be condemned. Forgive, and you will be forgiven"* (Luke 6:37, NKJV). *"For if you forgive men their trespasses, your Heavenly Father will also forgive you. But if you do not forgive men their trespasses, neither will your Father forgive your trespasses"* (Matthew 6:14-15, NKJV). Jesus gave us a perfect example of forgiveness when He said, *"Father, forgive them, for they do not know what they do..."* (Luke 23:34, NKJV). He forgave those who crucified Him at the cross because He did not want to be subject to un-forgiveness. Also, Jesus answered, *"Most assuredly, I say to you, whoever commits sin is a slave of sin"* (John 8:34 & 2 Peter 2:19, NKJV.). If we do not want to be under the control of un-forgiveness, we must forgive.

This part of the Lord's Prayer asks us to forgive others. It speaks about forgiveness among our associates, neighbors, friends, family and others. We also need God's forgiveness. We may even need to forgive ourselves for the mistakes we made in life. Self-forgiveness is very important because we cannot forgive others or God until there is forgiveness in our hearts. If you make a mistake, confess it to God or a friend, and then let it go. *"If you forgive, you also shall be forgiven"* (Luke 6:37, NKJV).

Jesus taught His disciples to forgive seventy-seven times seven. *"Peter came up to Him and said, Lord, how many times may my brother sin against me and I forgive him and let it go. [As many as] up to seven times. Jesus answered him, I tell you, not up to seven times, but seventy times seven!"* (Matthew 18:21-22, AMP). In other words, we must continue to forgive without limit. However, it does not mean to place ourselves in the same situation to be hurt all over again. This would be foolish. On the contrary, we ought to be wise, as commanded by Jesus Christ.

There is a difference between forgiveness and relationship. We have defined forgiveness as simply a choice to cancel a debt owed. It is a process to grant free pardon and give up all claims on a balance owed. By its nature, there is no requirement for forgiveness; it should be given freely. *"Freely you have received, freely give"* (Matthew 10:8b, NIV).

Relationship, however, is different. There is a prerequisite for relationship: repentance. *"I tell you, no! But unless you repent, you too will all perish"* (Luke 13:3, NIV). God loves us unconditionally and has extended forgiveness to all who wants to receive it; however God will not have a relationship with an unrepentant person.

Likewise, we should forgive those who transgress against us, but we should not restore relationship until we can see evidence of change. We must know for sure that the other party has changed and desires to return to relationship with us before we put ourselves at risk again. This is a very sensitive situation; we highly recommend that you follow the leading of the Holy Spirit and the counsel of wise loved ones before restoring relationship again.

Forgiveness is a choice even when we remember the pain; we can choose to forgive and move on. We understand that it is a difficult process, but all is possible with God. Forgiveness requires only one person, whereas relationship requires two. Even if the transgressor never asks for forgiveness or receives our forgiveness, we can still choose to forgive. Those who choose not to forgive carry the pain and become bound to it.

The greatest benefit to forgiveness is freedom. However, this freedom is not free. We must choose to seek it diligently to find it. Research has shown that un-forgiveness can cause psychological problems such as anxiety, depression and loneliness. The Bible concurs in the following verse, *"A cheerful heart is good medicine, but a crushed spirit dries up the bones"* (Proverbs 17:22, NIV).

Un-forgiveness and bitterness will crush bones! It is our prayer that you will practice forgiveness in your life, because forgiveness will help you live a peaceful, healthy and joyful life. Forgiveness is one of the keys to 'freedom living.' As you receive more of God's love in your heart, you will become more empowered to forgive.

"Lead us not into temptation, but deliver us from evil"

Here is a different translation of this statement: "Daily, we are being tempted, but, O God, deliver us from its evil!" (Anthony C. Deane, Canon of Worcester Cathedral, 1939). It is important to note that God does not tempt anyone; that is not His style. We are tempted by our sinful desires and the influence of others or the devil. When temptation is acted upon, it leads to sin (disobedience); and sin leads to death (James 1: 13-15). The devil assists in temptation by whispering sinful thoughts into our minds to disobey God's Word. We need to ask our Heavenly Father to help us resist temptation and deliver us from its evil.

In addition to reading the Bible and seeking God's help with temptations, we recommend that you surround yourself with loving people when you are being tempted. God often partners with people to help people. As a child of God, you have authority to resist the devil to make him flee from you. You can be hopeful when tested, because God promised to keep you safe. Also, He will not let you be tempted beyond your ability to endure. The following scriptures shed some light on how to resist temptations and the devil:

- *Submit yourselves, then, to God. Resist the devil, and he will flee from you* (James 4:7, NIV).

- *No temptation has overtaken you except what is common to mankind. And God is faithful; He will not let you be tempted beyond what you can bear. But when you are tempted, He will also provide a way out so that you can endure it* (1 Corinthians 10:13, NIV).

- *"Be sober, be vigilant; because your adversary the devil walks about like a roaring lion, seeking whom he may devour. Resist him, steadfast in the faith, knowing that the same sufferings are experienced by your brotherhood in the world"* (1 Peter 5:8-9, NKJV).

The Lord's Prayer is also known as the Disciples' Prayer. It is the initial prayer that Jesus taught His disciples. It has been the pattern for Christians' prayer ever since. This prayer is so profound that the words have been harmonized into song. Although it is great to memorize and sing the Lord's Prayer, it should not be used as a mere chant. The principles hidden in the words are what Jesus wanted to teach. If you follow the principles of this powerful prayer, you will be effective in your prayer life.

Chapter 5

THE 3 KEYS TO EFFECTIVE PRAYER

Years ago, my father worked in the construction field to provide for us. He helped construct and repair hundreds of buildings and roads in New York City. He would regale my brothers and I with innumerable stories about particular construction projects. One of the lessons I learned from his stories is that "wise builders build on solid foundations." He encouraged my siblings and me to build our lives on solid foundations such as faith, integrity, wisdom, education and hard work. No building structure can stand without a solid foundation. Likewise, effective prayer must be built upon a solid foundation. This chapter looks at three keys to building a solid foundation that foster intimacy with God through effective prayer.

There are prerequisites to building a solid foundation for effective prayer, so let's establish the primary prerequisite: *faith* in God. Why is faith important? Well, *"Without faith it is impossible to please God, because anyone who comes to Him must believe that He exists and that He rewards those who earnestly seek Him"* (Hebrews 11:6, NIV). We pray to God because we believe in Him. *"Only fools say in their hearts, "There is no God..."* *"But we know that there is only one God, the*

Father, who created everything, and we live for Him. And there is only one Lord, Jesus Christ, through whom God made everything and through whom we have been given life" (Psalm 14:1, Mark 12:32 & 1 Corinthians 8:6, NLT). Again, we pray to God because we have faith in Him.

God is a spiritual being. Therefore, we can only see Him through eyes of faith. Let's be honest: it is difficult to talk to a stranger, let alone an invisible God. It is hard to talk to a supernatural being that you cannot see. However, faith makes it possible for us to connect to God. In other words, "believing is seeing."

Faith is vital in prayer because it is impossible to know God without it. Note that it is not enough to just believe in God, but you must *act* on your faith. This scripture explains, *"You believe that there is one God. Good! Even the demons believe that—and shudder* His word. Jesus said to His followers, *"You are truly my disciples if you remain faithful to my teachings." "If you love me, obey my commandments"* (John 8:31 & John 14:15, NLT).

The three keys to effective prayer listed in this chapter will be of no value to you if you do not have a relationship with God. This book is written to help you strengthen your established relationship with

God. If you want your prayer life to be powerful, you must develop a relationship with God through faith.

God, I want to have a relationship with you. I believe in you and I believe in your son, Jesus. I believe that Jesus died on the cross for my sins. I believe that Jesus is the way, the truth, and the life. No one can come to you except through your Son, Jesus Christ. Thank you for sending Jesus to redeem me from sin and death. Please forgive my sins and give me the gift of eternal life. I invite you into my life and I give you my heart. I want to serve you for the rest of my life. Amen.

If you pray this prayer, we believe that you are a friend of God. Congratulations on the biggest decision of your life! We welcome you into the family of God! We want to hear from you to celebrate with you. We also want to offer you additional resources that will be helpful grow spiritually. Please contact us by visiting CoachJamesJustin.com or connect with us on social media!

After requesting a relationship with God through Christ, it's important to commit to *grow* in that relationship. *Commitment is the initial key for building an intimate relationship with God through effective prayer.* Intimacy cannot be established without a commitment. Commitment is the solid foundation for all intimate relationships.

There are different ways to define commitment; however, we like this one: Commitment is an act of love whereby an individual willingly agrees to perform an activity. The commitment of a parent to a child and a husband to a wife is similar to the one to God.

But in order to commit to God, we must make a conscious decision to trust and to love Him. It is like taking the marriage vows. This commitment must be from the heart. We must be willing to forsake all others and have no other gods in our life. We must be willing to keep our vows to God in good times and in bad times. This type of commitment is critical and must be established to foster effective prayer. There will be testing times in your relationship with God, and it is in *those* times that your commitment will sustain you. Your commitment tells God that He can trust you. It also shows that you are in it for the long haul. Your commitment will drive your desire to grow in relationship with God.

There are many reasons why it is difficult to commit to God and to others. From counseling others, we discovered that *fear* is a major reason why some people struggle with commitment. The fear of being hurt causes them to stay isolated from others. Opening the heart to relationship again may feel too risky for such a person. Therefore, in order to protect themselves they keep their hearts closed.

Past hurts can inhibit our ability to commit to God and to others. The human rationale encourages self-protection through emotional isolation. However God does not want us to protect ourselves by closing our hearts in relationships. When we isolate from others because of fear of getting hurt, we forfeit all opportunities to receive love.

Living on an emotional island is very lonely and **not** the way God intended for us to live. To reject relationships with others because of fear of getting hurt is to reject love. When we reject love, we reject God, for God is love. To overcome fear and receive love, we must become vulnerable to God and others. We must take a risk. When we open our hearts to God, he will heal those past hurts and restore us to wholeness.

Prayer is a wonderful way to open our hearts to God. As we express our hearts to God in prayer, he will heal our brokenness. As we allow him to heal us, our hearts will become soft again and we will become more receptive to commitment and love.

Low self-esteem is another reason why some people cannot commit to God, to others and even to themselves. They do not believe that they are good enough to be in a loving and committed relationship. They do not feel that they have anything to offer in a relationship. They are often so full of self-contempt that even though they may have much strength, they do not believe so. The strengths they have are hidden under their negative self-talk and image.

If this is your case, there is good news! The power of God can break the power of fear and low self-esteem over your life. You can ask God for help in prayer right now. We also recommend that you seek help from loving people or a professional Christian counselor. Mostly, we urge that you be patient. It takes time to build a committed relationship. As you continue to read the Bible and to talk to God, He will show you how to properly commit to Him and to others.

Another barrier preventing commitment to God is *un-repented sin.* Sin creates a wedge between us and Him. *"It's your sins that have cut you off from God. Because of your sins, He has turned away and will not listen anymore"* (Isaiah 59:1-2, NLT). What is sin? Sin is a theological term that refers to a thought or an act of disobedience to God's word. As humans, we were born into sin and subject to its consequences (Psalm 51:5 & Romans 6:23).

Therefore, we are all in need of God's loving grace (Romans 3:23). This saving grace is available to those who repent from their sins and accept Jesus Christ as Lord and Savior. *"If you confess with your mouth the Lord Jesus and believe in your heart that God has raised Him from the dead, you will be saved"* (Romans 10:9, NKJV).

In God's loving grace, He made it possible for us to receive forgiveness from sin and death. He gave His Son as the ransom for our sins (John 3:16). This means that God is the only one with the antidote to our sin virus. To be free from the power of sin and death, we need to go to the source. Jesus Christ is the source of life. He said, *"I am the way, the truth, and the life. No one comes to the Father except through Me"* (John 14:6).

Jesus has the power to forgive sins. He is ready to forgive those who repent. He forgave King David when he sin, and He is ready to do the same for you. You can read King David's prayer for forgiveness in Psalm 51:1-19.

Sin is a big deal to God. He hates all sins. Sin brings death to His creations. Keep in mind that He is the God of life. He is Holy and cannot take part in sin. God will never tolerate sin because of sin's destructive nature. He does not want His creation to stay in that state. He will not participate nor condone something so destructive to His children. *"For the wages of sin is death, but the gift of God is eternal life in Christ Jesus our Lord"* (Romans 6:23, NKJV).

While God hates sin, He loves His children. He does not want to be separated from His children.

You can be assured that God will not stop loving you even when you sin. However, He will not encourage you to continue living in sin. He is Holy and wants His children to be holy (Leviticus 20:26). He is always ready to resume relationship with us as soon as we walk away from that destructive nature and repent. Jesus explained this nature of God in the following story of the lost son:

A man had two sons. The younger son told his father, "I want my share of your estate now before you die." So his father agreed to divide his wealth between his sons. A few days later this younger son packed all his belongings and moved to a distant land, and there he wasted all his money in wild living. About the time his money ran out, a great famine swept over the land, and he began to starve. He persuaded a local farmer to hire him, and the man sent him into his fields to feed the pigs. The young man became so hungry that even the pods he was feeding the pigs looked good to him. But no one gave him anything. When he finally came to his senses, he said to himself, "At home even the hired servants have food enough to spare, and here I am dying of hunger! I will go home to my father and say, 'Father, I have sinned against both heaven and you, and I am no longer worthy of being called your son. Please take me on as a hired servant.'" So he returned home to his father. And while he was still a long way off, his father saw him coming. Filled with love and compassion, he ran to his son, embraced him, and kissed him. His son said to him, "'Father, I have sinned against both heaven and you, and I am no longer worthy of being called your son." But his father said to the servants, "Quick! Bring the finest robe in the house and put it on him. Get a ring for his finger and sandals for his feet. And kill the calf we have been fattening. We must celebrate with a feast, for this son of mine was dead and has now returned to life. He was lost, but now he is found." So the party began (Luke 15:11-24, NLT).

The loving father in this story never went after the son. Instead, he waited for his son to come back to him. He gave his son the power to choose how he wanted to live his life. It is the same with our Heavenly Father. God does not control our choices; He allows us to choose as we will. Although He will not participate in our destructive behaviors, God's arms are always open to take us back when we choose to return home. God's love and compassion is amazing. If you have not committed to God, now is a great time to get started!

If you walked away from Him; and have been contemplating coming home, do not wait one more second. Let's just do it now! If you are ready, you can pray this prayer and your Heavenly Father will open His arms to receive you:

God, I am sorry I walked away from you. I realize that my choice was not a good one. I chose not to listen to you and it caused both of us pain. Please forgive me, I am ready to change. I know that it will not be easy, but I am willing to trust you. I want to come home. I pray in Jesus name. Amen.

Remember that God wants an intimate relationship with all His children. This is a relationship of a lifetime! It is built upon a daily commitment, trust and honesty. For without these principles, no relationship can grow.

Honesty is the next key for building an intimate relationship with God through prayer. Being honest is being sincere or straightforward in thoughts, feelings and actions. It is like speaking from your heart to your best friend. When we pray earnestly it strengthens our commitment to God. This is what Jesus teaches:

And when you pray, you shall not be like the hypocrites. For they love to pray standing in the synagogues and on the corners of the streets, that they may be seen by men. Assuredly, I say to you, they have their reward. But you, when you pray, go into your room, and when you have shut your door, pray to your Father who is in the secret place; and your Father who sees in secret will reward you openly. And when you pray, do not use vain repetitions as the heathen do. For they think that they will be heard for their many words. Therefore do not be like them. For your Father knows the things you have need of before you ask Him (Matthew 6:5-8, NKJV).

In this scripture, Jesus teaches the importance of sincerity in prayer. Since God already knows our hearts, we can speak to Him freely. He is not intimidated by our questions or requests. You see God already knows all things; therefore it is best to always be honest. God is not concerned about doctrinal or political correctness. He wants the truth. Even if what you are feeling is not doctrinally correct, God can lead you to the truth if you are willing to be honest. Many of us are not really honest in our conversations with God because we are afraid. We fear that if we are really honest, we might be disrespectful. So we hide our true feelings behind false praise. This is called lip service. God does not want lip service; He wants our heartfelt thoughts and emotions, even if they are not pleasant.

We believe that the number one barrier to effective prayer is *insincerity. Insincerity is the state of being dishonest, untruthful, deceitful, hypocritical or unwilling to express the truth.* When it comes to prayer honesty is always the best policy. All of us are guilty of praying falsely at one point or another. One of the reasons is that we were not taught properly. Some of us were taught that we cannot express ourselves to God fully. We can only share the good news. For example, we were taught that we cannot tell God that we are mad or sad as a Christian. While this may be a religious view, it is not Biblically accurate. God loves us and wants an intimate relationship with His children. You cannot have an intimate relationship without the ability to express yourself. We recommend that you share your thoughts and feelings, behaviors and struggles with God. Even if you believe that your thoughts and feelings are out of control, you can pray for help. He is the best person for the job. He is all powerful.

The Bible teaches us to have self-control. If you need help in this area, you can pray about it today. The Holy Spirit is willing to show you how to control your emotions. The Holy Spirit will help you to grow in your relationship with God and help you to produce much fruit. You can read more about the fruits of the Holy Spirit in the book of Galatians chapter 5 verses 22-23.

As human beings, we have a *spirit*, a *soul* and a *body*. Emotions play a great part of the human soul. The soul includes the mind, the will and the emotions. In relationships, emotions help us identify our feelings toward one another and impact how we interact with others. We are all unique in how we express our emotions. Our emotions are neither good nor bad. However, what we do with them can be either good or bad. One of the jobs of our feelings is to warm us that we are safe or in danger. Sometimes our true feelings make us uncomfortable, because some of us categorize feelings as either good or bad. Other times, a feeling may give us a warning of danger ahead, but we may ignore it because we may not want to change.

As for our thoughts, we are sometimes ashamed or afraid of the evil they reveal. If we are not careful, our thoughts may cause us to act sinfully. We are all responsible for our own thoughts, feelings and actions. If we surrender our lives unto God, He is faithful to help us. It is always best to express ourselves to God and allow Him to lead us to the truth. He already knows our thoughts, feelings and behaviors before they are manifested. *"You know my downsitting and my uprising; you understand my thought afar off"* (Psalm 139:2, AMP).

Therefore, we do not need to hide anything from Him. The lesson is to be honest with your thoughts, feelings and actions. If you are sad, mad, happy or experiencing any other emotions, you should tell God. He has the power to change your mess and give you His best. When you fail to take control over your thoughts and feelings, you are likely to make a mess. For example, if I physically hurt someone because I am feeling angry, it is a sin and a criminal offense. I can be charged with assault and battery. Obviously, this is not an acceptable way of managing my anger. Instead of acting on my anger in this manner, I can wait until I am able to be civil and able to express my emotion effectively. There is nothing wrong with anger, but it must be released effectively. It must be managed according to the will of God. These scriptures share some light on how to deal with anger.

"In your anger do not sin," do not let the sun go down while you are still angry, and do not give the devil a foothold. Anyone who has been stealing must steal no longer, but must work, doing something useful with their own hands, that they may have something to share with those in need. Do not let any unwholesome talk come out of your mouths, but only what is helpful for building others up according to their needs, that it may benefit those who listen. And do not grieve the Holy Spirit of God, with whom you were sealed for the day of redemption. Get rid of all bitterness, rage and anger, brawling and slander, along with every form of malice" (Ephesians 4:26-31, NIV).

When you bring your thoughts and your feelings to God, He will give you the wisdom to handle them properly. We also recommend that you express your negative emotions to your Heavenly Father quickly. He has the answer that you need. He has the power to heal your spirit, soul and body. God's word has power. *"For the word of God is living and powerful, and sharper than any two-edged sword, piercing even to the division of soul and spirit, and of joints and marrow, and is a discerner of the thoughts and intents of the heart"* (Hebrews 4:12, NKJV). The ability to express unpleasant emotions in a relationship is a great indicator of the trust level. Your ability to tell God your true feelings shows how much you trust Him. This brings us to our final key, trust.

Trust is the third essential key in building intimacy. No relationship can survive without it. Trust is to a relationship as oxygen is to the body. All loving relationships must be based on trust in order to grow and thrive. What is trust? *Trust is a firm reliance on the integrity, ability, or character of a person or thing.* Why trust God. The answer is really simple because He is trustworthy. You can trust that God will do what He says. *"God is no mere human! He doesn't tell lies or change His mind. God always keeps his promises"* (Numbers 23:19-19, CEV). In fact, everything He commands always comes to pass. He promised to bless Abraham and he was a blessed man. The same will be true for you. If God says, He will bless you, you can be sure of His Word. The Bible contains many examples of God's trustworthiness. He always comes through. He never fails. He is always there even if you do not feel Him. The fact that the sun rises every morning is a sign that you can trust God to keep his word.

The Bible commands us to trust God. Let us take a look at this scripture, *"Trust in the LORD with all your heart, and lean not on your own understanding; In all your ways acknowledge Him, and He shall direct your paths"* (Proverbs 3:5-6, NKJV). Trust is so important that God made it into a commandment. God's direction for our lives will be clearer as we trust Him. When we pray, we must trust. Otherwise, our prayer will be meaningless. Trust will build our faith and strengthen our commitment to God. More importantly, trust will bring us closer to God.

Trust is both an emotional and a rational act. Emotionally, it is where we expose our vulnerabilities openly to people and believe they will not take advantage of our honesty. Rationally, it is where we have calculated the probabilities of gain and loss based on previous experiences and data that leads to the conclusion that the person in question will behave appropriately. We are learning to trust God daily. We realize that it is best to obey God than to rely on our limited knowledge and wisdom. However, God wants us to trust Him openly and willingly. Trust must be earned and learned over time.

Now, it is our choice to trust. We know that for some people it is difficult to trust God. They do not even trust a visible being like a spouse or a friend. Therefore, it is harder to trust an invisible and supernatural being that they cannot see.

For many, mistrust is often a result of disappointments, rejection, heartbreaks and trauma. If this is your case, there is always hope for positive change. God can heal your heart and restore your soul. He is the great physician. As you seek healing for your spirit, soul and body, we recommend meditating on these scriptures (Isaiah 40:29, 53:5, 61:1-5; Psalm 147:3 & Jeremiah 30:17). If your healing has not yet come, do not give up; keep on trusting God. Tomorrow may be your time and season. Since God is all powerful and loving, you can trust Him in everything.

In our Freedom Living Seminars, one of the principles that we teach is: "If you change your mindset, you will change your life." It is really true, however, as we all know change is always challenging. The process of changing a mindset is not an easy task, but it is possible for those who believe it. With God and your willingness, you can change any negative mindset in your life. You will need to open your heart to God and to other dependable and loving people. As you learn to build relationships with trustworthy people, you will learn to trust again. If you have been hurt and have a difficult time to trust, we invite you to meditate on the following prayer:

Heavenly Father, please teach me how to trust you, myself and others. It is difficult to trust when I'm in pain, when I feel that you are not listening and when others disappoint me. As I go through life transitions, please show me how to trust and open my heart to those who really care. For I know that trust is an essential tool for effective relationships and I want an intimate relationship with you and those who are around me. Thank you for helping me with trust and helping me to practice it. Amen.

We hope that the information given in this book will help strengthen your prayer life and ultimately your relationship with God. Prayer is like a muscle. The more you use it the stronger it will become. The more you talk to God, the more He will draw near to you. As you develop your commitment, maintain your honesty and build your trust in God, you will develop an intimate relationship with your creator.

Chapter 6

TOP 20 PRAYERS OF ALL TIME

The Lord's Prayer

Our Father which art in heaven, Hallowed be thy name. Thy kingdom come, thy will be done in earth, as it is in heaven. Give us this day our daily bread. And forgive us our debts, as we forgive our debtors. And lead us not into temptation, but deliver us from evil: For thine is the kingdom, and the power, and the glory, forever. Amen.

(Matthew 6:9-13).

Psalm 23 Prayer

The Lord is my shepherd; I shall not want. He makes me lie down in green pastures; he leads me beside still waters; he restores my soul. He leads me in right paths for his name's sake. Even though I walk through the valley of the shadow of death, I fear no evil; for you are with me; your rod and your staff--they comfort me. You prepare a table before me in the presence of my enemies; you anoint my head with oil; my cup overflows. Surely goodness and mercy shall follow me all the days of my life, and I shall dwell in the house of the Lord

forever.

(Psalms 23:1-6)

The Abundance Life Prayer

Today I live in abundance in my Spirit, Soul, Body and all areas of my life!

Everything and everyone I need to create this kind of abundance come to me in effortless ease! For it is God's pleasure to lavish his blessings over me!

As a result, all that come in contact with me will be blessed!

(Dr. Lauretta Justin)

The Prayer of Jabez

"Oh that you would bless me and enlarge my territory!

Let your hand be with me and keep me from harm, so that it will not hurt me."

(1 Chronicles 4:10)

Make Me an Instrument of Your Peace

Lord, make me an instrument of your peace.
Where there is hatred, let me sow love,
Where there is injury, pardon
Where there is doubt, faith,
Where there is despair, hope,
Where there is darkness, light,
Where there is sadness, joy.
O Divine Master, grant that I may not so much
seek to be consoled as to console,
not so much to be understood as to understand,
not so much to be loved, as to love;
for it is in giving that we receive,
it is in pardoning that we are pardoned,
it is in dying that we awake to eternal life.

(St. Francis of Assisi)

Prayer before meals

O Lord, bless this food to our use,
and us to your service;
make us grateful for all your mercies,
and mindful of the needs of others. Amen.

Christ Be With Me

Christ with me, Christ before me, Christ behind me,
Christ in me, Christ beneath me, Christ above me,
Christ on my right, Christ on my left,
Christ where I lie, Christ where I sit, Christ where I arise,
Christ in the heart of everyone who thinks of me,
Christ in the mouth of every one who speaks to me,
Christ in every eye that sees me,
Christ in every ear that hears me.
Salvation is of the Lord.
Salvation is of the Christ.
May your salvation, Lord, be ever with us.

(St. Patrick)

Prayer for Aid Against Perils

Be our light in the darkness, O Lord, and in your great mercy defend us from all perils and dangers of this night; for the love of your only Son, our Savior Jesus Christ. Amen.

(Book of Common Prayer 1979)

Evening Family Prayer

Lord, behold our family here assembled.
We thank you for this place in which we dwell,
for the love that unites us,
for the peace accorded to us this day,
for the hope with which we expect the morrow;
for the health, the work,
the food and the bright skies
that make our lives delightful;
for our friends in all parts of the earth. Amen.

(Robert Louis Stevenson)

Prayer for Comfort and Hope

Grant unto us, Almighty God, in all time of sore distress, the comfort of the forgiveness of our sins. In time of darkness give us blessed hope, in time of sickness of body give us quiet courage; and when the heart is bowed down, and the soul is very heavy, and life is a burden, and pleasure a weariness, and the sun is too bright, and life too mirthful, then may that Spirit, the Spirit of the Comforter, come upon us, and after our darkness may there be the clear shining of the heavenly light; that so, being uplifted again by Thy mercy, we may pass on through this our mortal life with quiet courage, patient hope, and unshaken trust, hoping through Thy loving-kindness and tender mercy to be delivered from death into the large life of the eternal years. Hear us of Thy mercy, through Jesus Christ our Lord – Amen.

(George Dawson)

Prayer for Comfort in Christ

Christ is shepherd over you,
Enfolding you on every side.
Christ will not forsake you, hand or foot,
Nor let evil come near you.
Amen

Prayer for God's Hope

God is our hope and strength, a very present help in trouble.

Therefore, will we not fear, though the earth be moved, and though the hills be carried into the midst of the sea;

Though the waters thereof rage and swell, and though the mountains shake at the tempest of the same.

There is a river, the streams whereof make glad the city of God, the holy place of the tabernacle of the Most High.

(Psalms 46:1-4)

Prayer for Trust in Jesus

O Christ Jesus,
when all is darkness
and we feel our weakness and helplessness,
give us the sense of Your presence,
Your love, and Your strength.
Help us to have perfect trust
in Your protecting love
and strengthening power,
so that nothing may frighten or worry us,
for, living close to You,
we shall see Your hand,
Your purpose, Your will through all things.

(St. Ignatius of Loyola)

Prayer for Forgiveness

Have mercy on me, O God, according to your steadfast love; according to your abundant mercy blot out my transgressions. Wash me thoroughly from my iniquity, and cleanse me from my sin.

For I know my transgressions, and my sin is ever before me. Against you, you alone, have I sinned, and done what is evil in your sight, so that you are justified in your sentence and blameless when you pass judgment. Indeed, I was born guilty, a sinner when my mother conceived me.

You desire truth in the inward being; therefore teach me wisdom in my secret heart. Purge me with hyssop, and I shall be clean; wash me, and I shall be whiter than snow. Let me hear joy and gladness; let the bones that you have crushed rejoice. Hide your face from my sins, and blot out all my iniquities.

Create in me a clean heart, O God, and put a new and right spirit within me. Do not cast me away from your presence, and do not take your Holy Spirit from me. Restore to me the joy of your salvation, and sustain in me a willing spirit.

(Psalms 51)

Prayer for Protection

The Lord is my light and my salvation—whom shall I fear?

The Lord is the stronghold of my life—of whom shall I be afraid?

When evil men advance against me to devour my flesh,

when my enemies and my foes attack me,

they will stumble and fall.

Though an army besiege me, my heart will not fear;

though war break out against me, even then will I be confident.

(Psalms 27:1-3)

Prayer for Healing

Almighty and merciful Father, by the power of your command, drive away from me all forms of sickness and disease. Restore strength to my body and joy to my spirit, so that in my renewed health, I may bless and serve you, now and forevermore.

Prayer for Times of Fear

Almighty God, the Refuge of all that are distressed, grant unto us that, in all trouble of this our mortal life, we may flee to the knowledge of Thy lovingkindness and tender mercy; that so, sheltering ourselves therein, the storms of life may pass over us, and not shake the peace of God that is within us. Whatsoever this life may bring us, grant that it may never take from us the full faith that Thou art our Father. Grant us Thy light, that we may have life, through Jesus Christ our Lord. Amen.

(George Dawson)

Prayer for Peace

O Lord, my God, grant us your peace; already, indeed, you have made us rich in all things!

Give us that peace of being at rest, that Sabbath peace, the peace which knows no end.

(St. Augustine)

The Serenity Prayer

God grant me the serenity to accept the things I cannot change; courage to change the things I can;

and wisdom to know the difference.

Living one day at a time; enjoying one moment at a time; accepting hardships as the pathway to peace;

taking, as He did, this sinful world as it is, not as I would have it; trusting that He will make all things right if I surrender to His Will; that I may be reasonably happy in this life and supremely happy with Him forever in the next.

Amen.

(Reinhold Niebuhr, 1892-1971)

Children's Bedtime Prayer

Now I lay me down to sleep,
I pray the Lord my soul to keep:
May God guard me through the night
And wake me with the morning light.
Amen.

CONCLUSION

Prayer is the process of communicating with God. If you can talk with your best friend, you can talk with God. Prayer is a powerful force that will transform your life as you use it to build your spiritual health.

The power of prayer is available to all of God's children; however not all His children know how to tap into this power source. The secret is found in building trust and a personal relationship with God. God wants you to communicate with him daily.

He already knows your needs, hopes, desires and fears, but He wants to hear about them from you. That's because he desires an intimate relationship with you where you not only talk to him but also listen as he gently speak into your heart. As you learn to trust him with all your heart, you'll discover the awesome power prayer can release in your life.

NOTES

What is prayer?

Prayer is a heartfelt communication between people and God. For more details, read chapter two of this book. The acronym F.A.C.T.S is a great way to remember the meaning of prayer. Prayer must be based on FAITH (Hebrews 11:1 & Romans 10:17), it is ADORATION (Psalms 95:6), it is CONFESSION (1 John 1:9, Psalm 51, James 5:16), it is THANKSGIVING (1 Thessalonians 5:16-18 & Psalms 100) and it is SUPLICATION ((1 John 5:14-15).

What is *Salvation?*

Salvation is the act of being delivered from sins and its consequences. *"For everyone has sinned; we all fall short of God's glorious standard. Yet God, with undeserved kindness, declares that we are righteous. He did this through Christ Jesus when he freed us from the penalty for our sins, for the wages of sin is death, but the free gift of God is eternal life through Christ Jesus our Lord"* (Romans 3:23-24 & 6:23, NLT).

Steps to Salvation

1. Understand that God loves you and desires to give you eternal life.

    - *""For God loved the world so much that he gave his one and only Son, so that everyone who believes in him will not perish but have eternal life"* (John 3:16, NLT).

    - *"The thief does not come except to steal, and to kill, and to destroy. I have come that they may have life, and that they may have it more abundantly"* (John 10:10, NKJV).

2. Acknowledge that your sins separate you from God and that you need a Lord and Savior.

    - "Your iniquities have separated you from your God; your sins have hidden his face from you, so that he will not hear" (Isaiah 59:2, NIV).

3. Accept Jesus Christ as Lord and Savior and that He is God's only provision to salvation.

    - "God showed his great love for us by sending Christ to die for us while we were still sinners" (Romans 5:8, NLT).

    - "Christ suffered for our sins once for all time. He never sinned, but he died for sinners to bring you safely home to God. He suffered physical death, but he was raised to life in the Spirit" (1 Peter 3:18, NLT).

- "For there is only one God and one Mediator who can reconcile God and humanity—the man Christ Jesus" (1 Timothy 2:5, NLT).
- Jesus answered, "I am the way and the truth and the life. No one comes to the Father except through me" (John 14:6, NIV). .
- "If you confess with your mouth the Lord Jesus and believe in your heart that God has raised Him from the dead, you will be saved" (Romans 10:9, NKJV).
- We believe that you are ready to pray the following prayer:

Lord Jesus, I believe that you are the way, the truth, and the life. No one can go to heaven except through you. I believe you are the Son of God. Thank you for dying on the cross for my sins. Please forgive my sins and give me the gift of eternal life. I ask you in to my life and want you to be my Lord and Savior. I want to serve you for the rest of my life. Amen.

If you prayed this prayer, we believe that you have received God's eternal life. You are a friend of God and a citizen in His kingdom. Congratulations on the biggest decision of your life! We welcome you in the family of God! We would like to hear from you to celebrate with you and to share some resources that can be helpful in your new journey. Please visit us online at CoachJamesJustin.com!

- We encourage you to find a local Bible based church for fellowship, worship and to celebrate your new decision.
- Get baptize as a symbol of your faith.
- Read the Bible, pray and ask as many questions as you can.

The 5 eternal benefits of being in the family of God

As children of God, you have a guaranteed inheritance, no one can take it from you, because it is reserved for you in Heaven (1 Peter 1:3-5, NKJV). In a recent sermon, I preached on these five eternal benefits of being in God's family. These five benefits are available to all God's children:

First, you will be with God forever. *"Let not your heart be troubled; you believe in God, believe also in Me. In My Father's house are many mansions; if it were not so, I would have told you. I go to prepare a place for you. And if I go and prepare a place for you, I will come again and receive you to Myself; that where I am, there you may be also. And where I go you know, and the way you know"* (John 14:1-4, NKJV).

Second, you will have victory over death and the problems of life. *"I will ransom them from the power of the grave; I will redeem them from death. O Death, I will be your plagues! O Grave, I will be your destruction! Pity is hidden from My eyes"* (Hosea 13:14, NKJV). *"These things I have spoken to you, that in Me you may have peace. In the world you will have tribulation; but be of good cheer, I have overcome the world"* (John 16:33, NKJV).

Third, you will be changed completely and be like Christ. *"Beloved, now we are children of God; and it has not yet been revealed what we shall be, but we know that when He is revealed, we shall be like Him, for we shall see Him as He is"* (1 John 3:2, NKJV).

Fourth, you will get to share in Christ's glory. *"The Spirit Himself bears witness with our spirit that we are children of God, and if children, then heirs— heirs of God and joint heirs with Christ, if indeed we suffer with Him, that we may also be glorified together"* (Romans 8:16-17, NKJV).

Fifth, you will be rewarded. *"... Be faithful until death, and I will give you the crown of life"* (Revelation 2:10, NKJV). *"And whatever you do, do it heartily, as to the Lord and not to men, knowing that from the Lord you will receive the reward of the inheritance; for you serve the Lord Christ"* (Colossians 3:23-24, NKJV). *"I have fought the good fight, I have finished the race, I have kept the faith. Now there is in store for me the crown of righteousness, which the Lord, the righteous Judge, will award to me on that day—and not only to me, but also to all who have longed for his appearing"* (2 Timothy 4:7-8, NKJV).

In addition to the five eternal benefits listed above, there are other blessings that God wants His children to enjoy while on earth. For example, He promised to provide all of their needs according to His riches (Philippians 4:19). He promised to bless them as recorded in the book of Deuteronomy chapter 28 verses 1-14. *"The blessing of the LORD brings wealth, and he adds no trouble to it"* (Proverbs 10:22, NIV). God wants His children to have power, love and sound mind (2 Timothy 1:7). He wants them to grow (Genesis 1:28). He wants us to enjoy the fruit of the Holy Spirit. *"But the fruit of the Spirit is love, joy, peace, longsuffering, kindness, goodness, faithfulness, gentleness, self-control. Against such there is no law"* (Galatians 5:22-23, NKJV). God wants His children to be rooted and established in love (Ephesians 3:17).

We do not have to wait until we get to heaven to enjoy God's blessings. We can start enjoying them here on earth. God's blessings include our family, friends, health, the air, the flowers and even your job. As God's children, we have full access to His blessings; we simply need to ask Him in prayer. As we continue to build your relationship with God, He will teach us how to access His blessings. When we pray, we must *believe* and take positive action toward what we desire. *"Therefore I say to you, whatever things you ask when you pray, believe that you receive them, and you will have them"* (Mark 11:24, NKJV).

ABOUT THE AUTHORS

PASTOR JAMES JUSTIN

A born leader, James Justin hasn't let any obstacles stand in his way. And he has the skills to make sure your obstacles are broken and no longer stand in your way.

"It's my passion to inspire and help you transform, optimize and accelerate your life! This passion led me to earn my master's degree in the field of counseling and dedicate my life to speaking, coaching and helping people like YOU for over 20 years!"

James Justin is an entrepreneur, ordained minister, speaker, author and life coach. He earned his Masters of Social Work (MSW) degree from Boston College, and his Bachelors of Social Work (BSW) degree from Eastern Nazarene College in Quincy, Massachusetts. In 2011, James and his wife Dr. Lauretta co-authored and published their first book "Express Yourself!" In 2013, James published his solo book project titled "How to Develop Meaningful Relationships!" Both titles are available on his website or where ever books are sold.

James is the founder of Freedom Reign Church. He's a professor and consultant at Faith Christian University. He teaches in the Counseling Department. He worked as a professional counselor for the State of Florida for 7+ years prior to pursuing his passion and his dream–to help and makes an impact in the private sector.

James and Dr. Lauretta Justin are the proud parents of 3 incredible and very active boys – Nathan, Sean, and Joshua. James and Dr. Lauretta spend the majority of their free time focusing on "the boys" (in other words, trying to keep up with them)!! He enjoys reading, writing and hanging out with family and friends!

James is committed to helping create transformational growth with each and every one of his clients. He's available to help you achieve extraordinary results. Visit CoachJamesJustin.com to contact James!

DR. LAURETTA JUSTIN

Dr. Lauretta is known by her patients as the most caring, passionate, and dedicated eye doctor. Her mission is to Mentor, Empower, and Care for people with excellence in a refined atmosphere!

Dr. Lauretta Justin is an entrepreneur, speaker, author and singer! She is the founder, President and CEO of Millennium Eye Center where she practices optometry. She is the co-author of the 2011 book "Express Yourself!" In 2015, she released her debut Christmas music album titled, "The Spirit of Christmas!"

Dr. Lauretta is married to James Justin, her high school sweetheart, and together they have 3 sons. She enjoys reading, singing, playing with her family, and shopping for shoes!

Visit MillenniumEyeCenter.com or call 407-292-9812 to contact Dr. Lauretta Justin!

THE POWER OF PRAYER

Do you sometimes feel like you don't know what to pray for? Do you ever wonder if God is listening when you pray? Do you sometimes wish you knew how to use the power of prayer to change you, your relationships and your life?

The truth is the power of prayer is available to all of God's children; however not all His children know how to tap into this power source. The secret is found in building trust and a personal relationship with God. He wants you to communicate with him daily. He already knows your needs, hopes, desires and fears, but He wants to hear about them from you. That's because he desires an intimate relationship with you where you not only talk to him but also listen as he gently speak into your heart. As you learn to trust him with all your heart, you'll discover the awesome power prayer can release in your life. That is what this book is all about.

WHAT READERS ARE SAYING:

"I love this book! It's short and easy to read!"
–Kim Phillips

"I was not a big fan of prayer until I read this book. It inspired me to pray and it showed me the benefits of prayer."
–Josh Adams

"Thank you James and Lauretta for making prayer simple!"
–Maria Johnson

For more information, visit CoachJamesJustin.com!

www.ingramcontent.com/pod-product-compliance
Lightning Source LLC
Chambersburg PA
CBHW031552040426
42452CB00006B/274